Senryu

by Marc Awodey

minimal press edition
2008

also by Marc Awodey:
Telegrams from the Psych Ward and other poems
(1999)
New York, a haibun journey (2003)
95 Theses: Art and Machine (2004)
Senryu and Nudes (2008)

Verses in this collection were first published in
Senryu and Nudes (Kasini House 2008)
available through Kasini House Books
http://www.kasinihouse.com/books/. The
sequences *New York fragments, Broadway*,
and *Brooklyn* were first published in
New York, a haibun journey (WPC-Minimal
press 2003) available on Amazon.com,

Introduction is written by Janaka Stucky of
Black Ocean Press in Boston.
www.blackocean.org

SENRYU

Introduction

Perhaps my earliest encounter with Marc's
poetry was watching and hearing him compete
in a Head-to-Head haiku competition, in which
he took home the title of National Champion.
Fittingly, the verse he won the final round
with was more of a senryu than a haiku, and
it's included in this book:

swans are nasty birds
they honk,   bite
and chase children-
poets lie
*   for swans*

I say "fittingly" because nothing about Marc's
appearance in the competition was
conventional: a disheveled and bespectacled,
bearded man mumbling tiny bursts among a
bracket full of energetic and outspoken
younger competitors. As a young eccentric
poet in the audience, I left the event knowing
that I wanted to try my own hand at haiku,
and that I wanted Marc to be my sensei.

During the ensuing months I corresponded
with Marc about poetry, politics and art. By
the end of the following year I had won two
national haiku competitions myself. At a
competition in NYC, Marc showed his true
prowess as a sensei when he was defeated by
his own pupil: me. My year-long
apprenticeship with Marc in many ways
illustrates the strengths and pleasures that can
be found in his senryu. Consider this verse:

all these blank pages-
give me 100 more years
            then
i'll just give up

It contains a certain tension and paradox.
There is a sadness implied within, but an
awareness that also brings humor to that
sadness. Finally, the last line points back
toward the first line in a way that implies a
kind of inevitability. Marc's observations are
often cyclical, going from beginning to end to
beginning again. They are anti-temporal, but
not in the standard way a "haiku moment"
freezes times. Instead these senryu seem to be
simultaneously aware of what has happened
just before their genesis and how they will end
before they've even begun. Having given up at
the end, the blank pages in the beginning take
on an entirely new significance. In this way,
the last lines almost always shed a new kind of
perspective on the first ones.

   Perhaps the most compelling aspect to
Marc's senryu is the wry humor; they're too
sincere to be self-deprecating, yet at the same
time they don't take themselves too seriously.
Sometimes the humor is overt, but just as
often it is dry; almost deceptively subtle. The
reason for this is simple: Marc Awodey
doesn't care. His approach to senryu, to these
drawings and to their mutual subjects of life
and the human condition, in one of an
unpretentious and imperfect mind; they come

from an artist who is concerned with spontaneity and honesty more than he is with rules. There is no doubt that he knows what these rules are, but it's not just that he breaks them — it's that he doesn't even pay attention to them. Nonetheless there is that anti-temporal reflection at work, even as Marc observes his own artistic wreckage. In a telling moment he writes:

more paint on my shoes-
what picture had this color?
when did i paint it?

In a sense, these senryu and drawings all have the same subject: Marc Awodey. What we see in them again and again is not the object, but the artist. However this is not due to a lack of insight, or some clumsy interjecting embrace of subjectivity. It's because deep down Marc seems to see that there is no difference between the observed and the observer. That each continue to point toward each other, ad infinitum. Artist and object become one and the same in Marc's work. While each piece can tell its own story, in the end we come to understand something that Marc seems to have known all along:

write of the cosmos
or a desolate black gnat-
it makes no difference

Janaka Stucky
May, 2008

senryu

*

longing
for   heaven
i rubbed sand into my hair
and leapt at the clouds

*

"i don't like haiku!"
 so i wrote 1,000 verses
 just to be sure.

*

my woods grow darker-
is it these trees or
        those clouds
casting such kindness?

*

forgive me cricket,
one of us
must do this job-
and trout
      like you best

*

a praying mantis
leapt from a leaf to
      my head-
  she rode quite awhile

*

   we stroll as one
  through an imperfect
paradise
  discussing
weather

*

i rattle cages
but so many   are empty
it makes no difference

*

why risk so much?
squirrel jumps from branch
to tree
yet both are picked clean

*

how would i answer?
would i answer like
        an oak
questioned by lightning?

*

the cat and i
chase illusions -
   her's are bits of dust
mine are less clear

*

    it's astonishing!
  gray hairs
join my beard each night
when i'm most wakeful

*

more missed appointments-
      i must stop
scheduling things,
time is too unctuous

*

do not smile and write!
bearded wise men
      are austere
has no one taught you!

*

all these blank pages-
give me 100 more years
      then
i'll just give up

*

 an ant colony
cold beneath my shadow
  pleaded-
bring back the sun!

*

my wool socks are warm
these feet are shod
    well   enough
but her words-
sharp stones

*

 this scrap
so   unadorned
   i know
 it will be lost-
i rest,
so   knowing

*

some poets should
      write
about breakfast cereals
rather than hunger

*

write of the cosmos
or a desolate black gnat-
it makes no difference

*

academicians
with university jobs
buy nice
   umbrellas

*

more paint on my shoes-
what picture had this color?
when did i paint it?

*

say it in one breath-
so much can be said that way
and so much   more   lost

*

broken all the haiku rules
      sleepless
for three days
no-
   this ain't haiku

*

a gracious
old friend is so
generous with praise-
      her health worries me

*

my friend wrote about
  a lovely statue
in prague-
   "i gave her your book"

*

verbal jabs
        flutter
conversations ripple
  it's all   ping   pong
  to me

*

walking past cafes
a ghost fills
      my navy coat
its pockets- empty

*

novices question
authorities
analyze
dead horses abound

*

my dear humming bird
frantically
 sipping   nectar
rest with me awhile

*

  dear friend -
please keep reminding me
that i need to forget
about you

*

i once tried writing
fortunes for cookies
 but the job
had no future

*

swans are nasty birds
they honk,   bite
and chase children-
poets lie
        for swans

*

 no consummation
can surpass the mystery
of correspondence

*

verbal jabs
     erupt
conversations ripple
 it's all   ping
pong   to me

*

the lights
of her far off city
reflect
across clouds
       and
   photographs

*

i need
whiter leaves
and blacker pens every year
 as old age
      prospers

*

i've memorized the words
of an old letter
i can't bear to reread.

*

i once wrote about
 you
in an odd little poem
that's been erased

*

waiting for email-
i expect many words
that will never
             arrive

*

puppets spin together
 hung beneath
          polaris-
 you'll never leave
 me

*

there were once giants
but they were overwhelmed
   by
trivial concerns

*

the whole day is gone
i watched passing cars
     wrote poems-
a productive day

*

this lost
    old *poet-*
he can write for ten
         thousand
better than for one

*

each snowflake is one
dissolving like a secret
   to quench
swollen tongues

*

ghost- i implore you
this haunting decimates me
      please!
 make your demand!

*

transfiguration
happens
    every day-
  night is the true
miracle

*

i'm seeking a
calmer quieter
  universe-
  one with fewer
  stars

*

you won't recognize me
when we meet again
i now wear rougher
  clothes

*
your voice
is almost lost
    buried
beneath a paper
poem mountain

*

 you don't remember
i can't forget
 so we have a perfect
friendship

*

 bruised pears
rot on my lawn
dimpled by fat insects-
poor
neglected fruit

*

fading   into   sand
   i am a hermit crab
blind
        meticulous

*

i worked hard last night
but today is very hot
 my poems
 were ice

*

maybe even you
will like these poems...
or maybe
just the drawings.

*
the cat
walks on my keyboard
and i smile
  "kitty
thanks for writing!"

*

i've never had big dreams
just small
          visions
and a sad reality.

*

 a crumpled dollar bill
lays on my desk -
  another scrap of paper

*

this fertile winter
 is so confusing
   i wish it were cold
and dark

*

i've lost many dawns
to night
many songs to time
many friends to
death.

*

perfumed wives
who walk alone
to christmas parties
should stay out
till dawn

*
poetry
will always exist -
  only poets
  will ever read it

*
i was once saved
by an ambulance
  nice ride-
siren a bit noisy

*

i used to pick apples
  but i ate so many
no money was earned

*
a blackout
 dimmed my street
so i write
in candle light
and in shadows

*

my house seemed empty
so i made 100 paintings
 now it's too small

*

 writing outside
in the rain, i enjoy
watching my verses
 dissolve

*

a fruitless tree
 at least offers shade
  an old, leafless tree -
fire wood.

*

tea has been good for me lately
i write as it steeps, steams,
and darkens

*

sunny sidewalk -
my shadow is a compass
needle pointing
nowhere

*

my students worry
about painting in the rain
  poor youth!
why so frail?

*

a good friend who
unjustly lost her job
  now looks forward
to freedom

*

a man goes to work
 with coffee in his gut
queasy as the phone rings

*

i've deteriorated
   banged my face
into brick walls
            till i bled

*

a laughing Bodhisattva
friend of mine
   died
silently yesterday

*

all bad watercolors
should be rounded up!
 and thrown
into the sea!

*

everyone chitchats
at the coffee shop -
while i talk
 to my notebook

*

my pear trees
yielded no fruit last year,
  yet this year's blossoms
were fragrant

*

my drawings are as
imprecise as my verses
  but both have nice
lines

>

there's a recurring bird
  chirp
outside my window;
  my sole alarm clock

*

if the mail man brings
any more bills
i'll have to glue
the mail box shut!

*

to write a verse
about eye sight,
my nose had to almost touch
the page

*

the fog horn blows
a long vowel, tree frogs
short consonants-
  nice chitchat

*

a truck rumbles by -
someone already at work
 wakes me up at noon

*

went downtown early
  drinking coffee with milk now
it tastes like sunday

*

i'd rather read poetry
than write it
  writing is too
difficult

*

ezra pound
didn't really know chinese;
  i don't really know
english

*

i take a walk each night
 and think about
important things to forget.

*

cut off toes to fit the shoe?
go buy bigger shoes?
  no - i'll stay barefoot

*

i'd give a kidney
for senryu to be fiction
-   it's just too real

*

walking home from the play
i looked at the sky
and again   saw no stars

*

important art
needs to be more pretentious
 than mine could ever be

*

words
just a bunch of word
pay no mind what i've said

                forever,
                words

*

a thunderstorm
made my cat skittish
    so we both hid
under my desk

*
i can write no more
tonight has been very
    long   sleep
  brings my
        wages

New York fragments

*subways

a grand white cocoon
new york is an enigma
slowly unraveled

soft steel drums echo
slipping seams
of silver speed
-mine the underground

they fold newspapers
sew   daydreams into
next stop
BLKER station   stop-

all rise to retreat
uptown, downtown,
brooklyn bridge
slip out to the street

move quick off
their train
it's damp under manhattan
dripping
    from on high

subway fluorescence-
  washes
heaps of winter coat
  we sway like puffins

moving platform slides-
we have dodged the yellow line
two trains are aligned

a hall of girders
recedes into rattiness
        eastbound   void
westbound

tight as teeth,
riders   read   books
adjust their headphones
tittle-tattle
flirt

a grimy sleepwalk
 litter on low railroad ties
scuttles like a rat

a mourning dove preens
brooklyn bridge to 86th
costs
fourteen
minutes

*the met

   nearing the met's steps
feathers   frozen breath
        ascend
i dream of Cezanne

iridescent necks
bob to examine
pebbles-
    rose footed seekers

        blind
        roman portrait busts
        weep salt tears
      as they yearn
    for lost umber soil

arrogant Boranzino
   was a creamy youth
now dead   centuries

flesh loose on my bones
   naked before piety-
      flayed by El Greco

marble roman heads!
  weeping for red tuscany
  what could i have done?

*broadway

snow melts on my sleeve-
  onyx sky, metropolis
    shadows cross the page

idle car horns sing-
  new yorkers pass, gossiping
    paper bags rustle

street steam, sidewalk chill
  yellow taxis harmonize
    basso fire trucks growl

laced flakes embracing cinders
  melt on iron slabs
    falling feet recede

car alarm, brine breeze
  subway rumble, japanese-
    this is broadway's air

*brooklyn

rushing cirrus clouds
frame the brooklyn bridge
great inverted   gate-

silver sinews   to-and-fro
  ride the   brooklyn bridge
pluck Roebling's   zither

sacred   brooklyn bridge
  strung out over east river-
    sooty piers   eclipsed

your midwife-   Whitman
    brooklyn bridge
now your feet bear me
    beyond   vermont

gold on court street
hardware store-
    carroll gardens men
  count their bags of salt

all doors have two locks-
    spider skylight
catches sun
    we creak up four flights

  radiators tick
callous winds consume
        the street
neighbor ascends stairs

my first subway ride
was in montreal-
not here
i don't speak east coast

last weekend- boston
ginger brandy in my head
  -we all
    read poorly

why do you leave home
 my beard?
let the young dogs bark-
let the actors   act

last weekend- boston
bitter as the wind can get
    still feeling
    a chill

ashes fall on leaves
incandescent traveling
  damned-   infernal
trains

our morning hisses
wheeze   constant
steam pipe
 music-
   sore esophagus

tramp down damp court street
        delivery men
 argue
like winter starlings

i hear
the old God
push his elegant volume
  folks say-
    leaves of grass?

crumbs- but no bagel
still looking for something
  sweet
something near the page

thank you dear reader.

www.ingramcontent.com/pod-product-compliance
Lightning Source LLC
Chambersburg PA
CBHW031335040426

42443CB00005B/360